Spiritist Prayers

Spiritist Prayers

© Copyright 2019 by the United States Spiritist Council

Scripture quotations are from the ESV Bible (The Holy Bible, English Standard Version), copyright © 2001 by Crossway Bibles, a publishing ministry of Good News Publishers. Used by permission. All rights reserved.

ISBN 978-1948109123
LCCN 2019903188
Proofreading: Jussara Korngold
Book design: Helton Mattar Monteiro
Cover design: Mauro de Souza Rodrigues

International data for cataloging in publication (CIP)

K1829sp Kardec, Allan, 1804–1869.
Spiritist prayers: excerpted from the gospel according to Spiritism/ Allan Kardec. Translator: Helton Mattar Monteiro. – New York: United States Spiritist Council, 2019.
106 pp.; 15.24 cm.

Original title: Recueil de prières spirites (ch. xxviii, L'évangile selon le Spiritisme).

ISBN: 978-1948109123

1. Prayers. 2. Spiritism. 3. Christianity. I. Title. II. Title.

LCCN: 2019903188   DDC 133.93   UDC 133.7

1st edition, 1st print – March 2019

All rights reserved to
United States Spiritist Council
http://www.spiritist.us – info@spiritist.us

Manufactured in the United States of America

No part of this book may be reproduced or transmitted in any form or by any means, electronic or mechanical, including photocopying, recording, or by any information storage and retrieval system, without the prior permission in writing from the copyright holder.

The name "United States Spiritist Federation" is a trade mark registered of the United States Spiritist Council.

ALLAN KARDEC

Spiritist Prayers

Excerpted from the Gospel according to Spiritism

UNITED STATES SPIRITIST FEDERATION
NEW YORK
2019

"*Does prayer make humankind better?*

Yes. Those who enthusiastically and confidently pray have more strength to withstand the temptations of evil, and to get help from the good spirits sent by God to assist them in so doing. Such help is never refused when honestly asked for.'

a) How is it that some individuals who pray for long periods of time are sometimes repulsive, jealous, envious and harsh, lacking in compassion and mercy, and even extremely cruel?

What matters is how you pray, and not how much you pray. These individuals presume that all the virtue of prayer lies in its length and duration, and turn a blind eye to their own flaws. For them, prayer is an occupation, a means of passing their time, but not a true study of themselves. In these instances, it is not the remedy that is ineffective, but the manner in which it is employed."

Allan Kardec, *The Spirits' Book*, Q. 660

Contents

Preface – s.1 1

1 🌿 General prayers s. 2–10

The Lord's Prayer 7
At Spiritist Meetings 18
For Mediums 22

2 🌿 Prayers for oneself s. 11–41

To Guardian Angels and Protector Spirits 29
To ward off evil spirits 33
To ask for a fault to be corrected 35
To ask for strength to resist temptations 37
Thanksgiving for having overcome a temptation 39
Prayer for asking advice 39
In life's tribulations 41
Thanksgiving for a favor obtained 42
Act of submission and resignation 44
In face of imminent danger 47
Thanksgiving for having escaped a danger 48
When going to sleep 49
When sensing that one's life is coming to an end 50

3 🌿 Prayers for others s. 42–58

For someone in distress 57
Thanksgiving for a benefit granted to others 58
Prayer for our enemies and those who wish us evil ... 59

Thanksgiving for the good granted to our enemies 61
For the enemies of Spiritism 62
For a newly born child 66
For someone who is dying 69

4 ⚜ Prayers for the departed s. 59–76

For someone who has just passed away 73
For those departed who were dear to us 78
For distressed souls requesting prayers for themselves 80
For a deceased enemy 83
For a criminal 84
For someone who has committed suicide 85
For repentant spirits 87
For hardened spirits 88

5 ⚜ For the sick and the obsessed s. 77–84

Prayers for the sick 95
Prayers for the obsessed 98

Final remarks 106

Preface

1. SPIRITS HAVE ALWAYS SAID, "The form is nothing, the thought is everything. Everyone should pray according to their convictions and the manner that affects them most deeply; a good thought is better than many words with nothing from the heart within."

Spirits do not prescribe any definite formula of prayers; and when they give one, it is to help focusing the ideas, and especially to call attention to certain principles of the Spiritist tenets. They do so also to help people that are embarrassed to express ideas in their own words, because some individuals would not believe they were really praying, if their thoughts were not encased in some formula.

The selection of prayers contained in this book were chosen from messages mediumistically dictated by spirits under different circumstances – they have also dictated other prayers, using other words, appropriate to certain ideas or special cases, but the basic thought is the same, whatever the form they chose. The purpose of prayer is to elevate our souls to God; the diversity of formulas must not establish any difference among those who believe in God, and still less among followers of Spiritism, because God accepts them all without exception, when they are sincere.

We must not, therefore, consider this selection as an absolute form, but as a variety chosen among many instructions given by the spirits. It is an application of the principles of Gospel morality as developed in *The Gospel according to Spiritism*, a complement to its tenets on our duties toward God and neighbor, where all the principles of Spiritism are recalled.

Spiritism acknowledges as good the prayers deriving from all cults and religions, provided they are said from the heart and not only by the lips. Spiritism imposes itself on no one, and blames no one; God is too big to repel the voice that entreats or sings Its praises, one way rather than another. *Anyone who casts anathema against prayers that differ from one's own accepted form shows disregard for God's greatness.* To believe that God sticks to one formula for prayer is to try to attribute human pettiness and passions to It.

An essential condition for prayer, according to St. Paul,[1] is to be intelligible, so that it may speak

---

1 Allan KARDEC, *The Gospel according to Spiritism*, ch. XXVII, no. 16.

to our spirit. For that reason it is not enough for it to be said in a language understood by the person who prays; there are prayers in the vernacular that do not say much more to the thought than a foreign language would, and therefore do not reach the heart – the rare ideas they contain are often suffocated under an overabundance of words and the mysticism of language.

Being simple, concise and clear is the main quality required of a prayer, avoiding any unnecessary phraseology, or luxury of epithets, which are nothing but superfluous ornaments. Every word must have its meaning, awaken an idea, stir an inner fiber: in short, *it must make people think*. Only on this condition can prayer reach its goal, *otherwise it becomes mere noise*. Also, note the air of negligence and volubility with which they are said most of the time: we see lips moving; yet from the expression of the physiognomies to the very sound of the voices, one detects a mechanical act, purely external, to which the soul remains indifferent.

The prayers gathered in this selection are divided into five categories, namely:

1st) **General prayers**
2nd) **Prayers for oneself**
3rd) **Prayers for others (the living)**
4th) **Prayers for the departed**

5th) **Prayers for the sick and the obsessed**

In order to draw special attention to the purpose of each prayer, and to help clarify its scope, each of them are preceded by a preliminary statement or prologue, under the title of *Introduction*.

1
General prayers

› GENERAL PRAYERS

The Lord's Prayer

2.[2] Introduction

Higher-order Spirits have recommended placing the Lord's Prayer at the top of this selection, not only as a prayer, but as a symbol. Of all prayers, it is the one they put in the first rank, either because it comes from Jesus himself (Matthew 6:9-13 ESV), or because it can make up for all prayers according to the thought attached to it. It is the most perfect model of conciseness, a truly sublime masterpiece in its simplicity. Indeed, using every word in a most economical way, it sums up all human duties toward God, toward others, and toward ourselves. It contains a profession of faith, an act of worship and submission; an entreaty for things necessary for life; and the principle of charitable love. To say it on behalf of someone is to ask for what one would ask for oneself.

However, because of its brevity, the deep meaning contained in the few words which compose it escapes most of us. That is why it is generally said without focusing its thought in the applications of each of its parts; instead it is said as a formula whose efficiency

---

2 Section numbering starts with this book's *Preface*.

is proportional to the number of times it is repeated; or it is almost always ascribed one of three, seven or nine cabalistic numbers, drawn from an ancient superstitious belief in the virtue of numbers, which also employs it in operations of magic.

To make up for the vagueness which this concise prayer may leave in one's thought, and following the advice and the assistance given by good spirits, a comment has been added to each proposition which develops its meaning and shows its applications. According to the circumstances and the time available, one can thus say whether a simple or extended Lord's Prayer.

3. Prayer

*I. **Our Father in heaven, hallowed be your name.***

We believe in you, O Lord, because everything reveals your power and your goodness. The harmony of the universe testifies to wisdom, prudence, and foresight which far surpass all human faculties. The name of a supremely great and wise being is inscribed in all works of creation, from the blade of grass and the smallest insect to the stars moving in space, everywhere we see the proof of parental solicitude; that is why blind is the one who does not recognize you in your works, proud is the one who does not glorify you, and ungrateful is one who does not give you thanksgiving, praise and worship.

II. *Your kingdom come.*

Lord, you have given humans laws full of wisdom that would make them happy if they observed them. With these laws they could make peace and justice reign among them; they would help one another, instead of hurting one another as they do. The strong would support the weak instead of crushing them; they would avoid the evils engendered by all sorts of abuses and excesses. All the miseries of this world come from the violation of Your laws, because not a single offense can escape its fatal consequences.

To the brute, you have given instincts which mark out the limit of what is necessary, conforming to it mechanically. Yet to humans, besides instincts, you have given intelligence and reason; you have also given them freedom to observe or to break these godly laws which concern them personally – that is to say, to choose between good and evil, so that humans have merit or are held responsible for their actions.

No one can pretend ignorance of your laws, for in your parental foresight you have wished that they should be engraved in the conscience of each one of us, without distinction of worship or nation. Those who violate them are the ones who do not know you.

A day will come when, according to your promise, everyone will practice them. Then unbelief will have vanished; all will acknowledge you as the sovereign Master of all things, and the reign of your laws will be your kingdom on earth.

Deign, O Lord, to hasten your advent, giving all human beings the necessary light to lead them on the path of truth.

III. *Your will be done, on earth as it is in heaven.*

If submission is a duty of the child toward the parent, of the inferior toward the superior, how much greater should be the submission of the created being toward its Creator! To do your will, Lord, is to abide by your laws and submit, without grumbling, to your divine decrees. Humans will submit to them when they understand that you are the source of all wisdom, and that without you we cannot do anything; then we will do your will on Earth as the elect do in Heaven.

IV. *Give us this day our daily bread.*

Give us food to keep our body strong and healthy; also give us the spiritual food we need to develop our spirit.

Beasts find their own food; yet, because you have created humans free, they owe it to their own activities and the resources of their intelligence.

You said to us, humans, "By the sweat of your face you shall eat bread," (Genesis 3:19) by which you made work mandatory for us so that we can exercise our intelligence by seeking ways to provide for our needs and well-being, some by means of material work, others by means of intellectual labor. Without work we would remain stagnant and would not be able to aspire to the bliss of Higher-order spirits.

You support any individual of good will who trusts in you for basic necessities, but not those who delight in being idle and would actually like to obtain everything easily; or those who seek superfluous things.[3]

How many of them succumb by their own fault, by their carelessness, their improvidence; or by their ambition, and because they did not want to content themselves with what had been given to them! These have been the authors of their own misfortune, and have no right to complain, for they are being punished for their sins. But even such individuals are not abandoned by you because you are infinitely merciful. You extend a helping hand to them, as soon as, like the prodigal son, they sincerely come back to you.[4]

Before we complain of our fate, let us ask ourselves if it is not our own doing; to every misfortune that happens to us, let us ask ourselves if it would not

---

[3] Allan KARDEC, *The Gospel according to Spiritism*, ch. xxv.
[4] *Op. cit.*, ch. v, no. 4.

have been up to us to avoid it. But let us also admit that God has given us intelligence to draw ourselves out of the quagmire, and that it depends on us to make good use of it.

Since the law of labor is a necessary condition for humans on earth, give us courage and strength to perform it; give us also prudence, foresight and moderation, so that we do not end up losing the fruits of our work.

Give us, then, O Lord, our daily bread, that is to say, the means of acquiring through labor the things necessary to life, for no one has the right to claim anything superfluous.

If, for some reason, work is impossible for us, we trust in your divine providence.

If it enters into your plans to test our endurance by the severest privations, regardless of our efforts, we accept them as a just atonement for the faults we may have committed whether in this life or in a previous one. For you are just; we know that there are no unmerited sorrows, and that you never punish without cause.

Preserve us, O God, from harboring any thoughts of jealousy and envy of those who possess what we do not have, even of those who have the superfluous, when we lack what is necessary to life. Forgive them if they forget the law of charitable love and love of neighbor that you have taught them.[5] Also remove from our mind the thought of denying your justice, when witnessing the prosperity of the wicked and the misfortune that sometimes overwhelms good people. Now we know, thanks to new lights you have chosen to give us, that your justice is always fulfilled and not lacking to anyone; that the material prosperity of the wicked is as ephemeral as their corporeal existence, and that it will have terrible consequences, whereas the joy reserved for those who suffer with resignation will be eternal.[6]

🕯 v. *Forgive us our debts, as we also have forgiven our debtors.*

Each of our infractions of your laws, O Lord, is an offense to you, and a debt contracted that we will sooner or later have to pay. We ask for remission through your infinite mercy, under the promise of making an effort not to contract new ones.

You have made a specific law of charitable love; but charity does not consist only in assisting one's fellow soul in need; it is also in forgiveness and forgetfulness of offenses. By what right can we ask

---

5 Allan KARDEC, *The Gospel according to Spiritism*, ch. XVI, no. 8.

6 *Op. cit.*, ch. v, nos. 7, 9, 12, 18.

for your forgiveness, when we ourselves show none toward those whom we are complaining about?

Give me, God, the strength to stifle all resentment, all hatred and all grudges in my soul. *Let death not surprise me while I harbor a desire for revenge in my heart.* But if it is your will to take me to the other side, even on today, please may I be rid of all animosity when presenting myself before you, following the example of Jesus Christ, whose last words were a plea for mercy on behalf of his tormentors.[7]

The acts of persecution that the wicked make us endure are part of our earthly trials and must be accepted without grumbling, like any other trials. Let us not curse those who, by their wickedness, are paving the way to our eternal happiness; for you have told us, through the mouth of Jesus, "Blessed are those who are persecuted for righteousness' sake." Therefore, let us bless the hand that strikes and humbles us, because the bruises of the body strengthen our soul, and we will be lifted up in our humbleness.[8]

Blessed be your name, Lord, for teaching us that our lot is not irrevocably fixed after death; that we will find in other existences the means to redeem

---

7 Allan Kardec, *The Gospel according to Spiritism*, ch. x.
8 *Op. cit.*, ch. xii, no. 4.

and atone for our past faults, to accomplish in a new life what we were not able to achieve in the current one, for our advancement.[9]

Thus all the apparent anomalies of life are finally explained; light shed on our past and future, a striking sign of your sovereign justice and your infinite goodness.

🕯 VI. ***And lead us not into temptation, but deliver us from evil.***[10]

Give us, Lord, the strength to resist suggestions by evil spirits which try to turn us away from the path of good by raising bad thoughts.

Yet we ourselves are imperfect spirits which have incarnated on this earth to atone for past errors and improve ourselves. The first cause of evil lies in ourselves, and evil spirits will only profit from our bad inclinations, through which they can talk to us, in order to tempt us.

---

9 *Op. cit.*, ch. IV; ch. V, no. 5.

10 Some translations state: "And lead us not into temptation" (in Latin, *Et ne nos inducas in temptationem*). Well, this expression might suggest that temptation comes from God, which would voluntarily drive humans to evil – a blasphemous thought that would equate God with Satan, and could not have been what Jesus meant. Moreover, such misinterpretation would be in accordance with the popular belief in an alleged role played by demons. (See Allan KARDEC, *Heaven and Hell*, chapter X, "... of Demons").

Each imperfection is a door open to their influence, while they are helpless and give up all attempts against perfected beings. All we attempt to do to remove them will be useless, if we do not oppose them with an unshakable will for goodness, and an absolute renunciation of evil. It is therefore toward ourselves that we must direct our efforts, and then evil spirits will naturally pull away, for it is evil that draws them, while good repels them. (See further below, "Prayers for the sick and the obsessed.")

Support our weakness, Lord. Inspire in us, through the voice of our guardian angels and good spirits, the will to correct our imperfections, in order to shut any access to our souls by impure spirits. (See below, no. 11.)

Evil is not your work, Lord, for nothing bad can come from the source of all good. It is us who create evil by breaking your laws, and by the misuse we make of the freedom you have granted us. The day humans observe your laws, evil will disappear from the earth, as it has already disappeared in more advanced worlds.

Evil is no one's fatal necessity, and it seems irresistible only to those who abandon themselves to it with complacency. If we have the will to do it, we can also have a will of doing good; therefore, O God, we ask your assistance and that of the good spirits to resist temptation.

VII. **Amen (So be it).**[11]

May it please you, Lord, that our wishes be fulfilled! However, we bow to your infinite wisdom. On all things that we are not able to understand, may it be done according to your holy will, and not according to ours, because you only want our good, and you know better than us what is useful to us.

We raise this prayer to you, O God; on behalf of ourselves; we also raise it to you on behalf of all distressed souls, whether incarnate or discarnate, of our friends and our enemies as well, of all those who call for our assistance, and especially for ...[insert name].

We call for your mercy and blessings upon each and every one.

Note: At this point you can specify what to thank God for, and what to ask for ourselves or for others. (See below, prayers nos. 26 and 27.)

---

11 [Trans. note] In the French original, Allan Kardec makes mention of the traditional exclamation "So be it!" uttered at the end of the prayer but absent from original Gospel texts (though found in the *Authorised King James Version*).

At Spiritist Meetings

4. "FOR WHERE TWO OR THREE are gathered in my name, there am I among them." (Matthews 18:20)

5. Introduction

To be assembled in the name of Jesus does not mean that it does not suffice for us to be physically gathered, but rather to be spiritually united by a communion of thought and intention for goodness. Only then will Jesus be in the midst of the congregation, either he himself or the pure spirits which represent him. Spiritism makes us understand how spirits can be among us. They are there in their fluidic or spiritual bodies, and bearing the appearance that would make them known should they make themselves visible. The higher they are in hierarchy, the greater their radiant power; it is thus that they possess the gift of ubiquity and that they can be found in several places simultaneously: a single ray of their thought is enough for that.

With these words, Jesus wanted to show the effect of union and loving fellowship: the greater or lesser number of people is not what draws him closer – since, instead of two or three persons, he could have said ten or twenty – but the sentiment of charitable love which animates them toward one another. Now, for that, it suffices that two people are gathered. However, if these two people pray separately from each other, although still addressing Jesus, there is no communion of thought between them, especially if they are not moved by a sentiment of mutual benevolence. If they see one another with an evil eye, with hatred, envy or jealousy, the fluidic currents of their thoughts will repel each other instead of uniting in a common outpouring of empathy – and therefore *they will not be assembled in the name of Jesus;* Jesus will thus become only the *pretext* for such a meeting, and not its true motive.[12]

This does not imply that Jesus is deaf to the voice of one person; after all has he not said, "Everyone who calls upon the name of the Lord shall be saved" (Acts 2:21)? It is above all because he demands the love of neighbor, of which one can give more proof when together with many than in isolation; and that all selfish feelings drives him away. It follows that if, in a large assembly, only two or three persons are united in heart by a sentiment of true charitable love, while the others isolate themselves and focus in selfish or worldly thoughts, Jesus will be with

---

12 Allan KARDEC, *The Gospel according to Spiritism*, ch. XXVII, no. 9.

the first and not with others. It is not therefore the unison of words, songs or external demonstrations that constitute a meeting in the name of Jesus, but rather a communion of thoughts in accordance with the spirit of charitable love as personified in Jesus.[13]

Such must be the character of all serious Spiritist meetings, in which the participation of good spirits is sincerely desired.

6. Prayer

(AT THE BEGINNING of the meeting)

We pray to the Lord God Almighty to send us good spirits to assist us, to keep away those which might mislead us, and to give us the necessary enlightenment to distinguish truth from falsehood.

Also, move away all malevolent spirits, incarnate or discarnate, that might try to sow disunity among us, and turn us away from charitable love and love of neighbor. If some seek to break in here, let them find no access to the heart of anyone here present.

Good spirits that design to come and educate us, make us receptive to your advices; turn us away from all thoughts of selfishness, pride, envy, and jealousy; inspire us with indulgence and benevolence toward our present or absent fellow beings, whether

---

13 Op. cit., ch. x, nos. 7 and 8; ch. xxvii, nos. 2, 3, 4.

friends or foes. Finally, among the sentiments that shall animate us, please allow us to recognize your salutary influence.

Give the mediums, whom you will entrust with the task of conveying your teachings, awareness of the sacred mandate bestowed upon them, and seriousness in what they are about to perform, so that they invest it with the necessary intensity and inner retreat.

If, in the assembled group, there are people who were drawn by other feelings other than that of goodness, open their eyes to the light, and forgive them, as we ourselves forgive them for coming with bad intentions.

In particular, we pray to the Spirit ... [insert name], our Spiritual Guide, to assist and watch over us.

7. (AT THE END of the meeting)
We thank the good spirits that have kindly come to communicate with us, and also ask them to help us put into practice the teachings they have conveyed to us. Please make it so that, when leaving here, each one of us feels strengthened in the practice of good and love of neighbor.

For Mediums

8. "AND IN THE LAST DAYS IT SHALL BE," God declares, "that I will pour out my Spirit on all flesh, and your sons and your daughters shall prophesy, and your young men shall see visions, and your old men shall dream dreams; even on my male servants and female servants in those days I will pour out my Spirit, and they shall prophesy." (Acts 2:17–18)

9. Introduction

The Lord determined that light should be available to every human being, and penetrate everywhere through the voice of the spirits, so that everyone could obtain the proof of immortality. It is for this purpose that spirits manifest themselves today in all corners of the world, and mediumship; as one of the signs of the fulfillment of predicted times; is discovered in persons of all ages and walks of life, both in men and women, in children and among the elder population.

To learn the things of the visible world and to discover the secrets of material nature, God gave humans the bodily eyesight, the senses, and special instruments. With the telescope we look into deep space, and with the microscope we have discovered the world of the infinitely small. To penetrate the invisible world, God has given us mediumship.

Mediums are interpreters responsible for conveying to fellow humans the teachings of the spirits; or rather, *they are the material organs by which the spirits express themselves so as to render themselves intelligible to humans*. Their mission is holy because it aims at opening the horizons of eternal life.

The spirits come to educate humans about their future destinies, in order to bring us back to the path of good, and neither to spare us the material work that we all must accomplish here below for our own advancement, nor to stimulate human greed and ambition. This awareness should pervade all mediums, so that they do not misuse their faculty. Those who understand the solemn seriousness of the mandate with which they are entrusted, perform it religiously, Their conscience would reprehend them for the sacrilegious act of deriving fun or turning into entertainment – whether for themselves or for others – a faculty bestowed upon them for a purpose so serious, which actually puts them in touch with beings beyond the grave.

As interpreters of spirit teachings, mediums should play an important role in the moral transformation that is taking place now; the services they can render are dependent on the good direction they give to their mediumistic faculties, whereas those who persist in wrong conduct are more harmful than helpful to the cause of Spiritism. By the bad impression they cause, they retard quite a few conversions. This is why they will be held accountable for the use they have made of a faculty which has been given to them for the good of their fellow human beings.

The mediums that want to keep the assistance of good spirits must work on their own improvement. Whoever wishes to see their mediumistic faculties grow and develop must themselves grow morally, and avoid anything that might detract from their providential purpose.

If good spirits sometimes use imperfect instruments, it is to give good advice and try to bring them back to the good path. However, if they find hardened hearts, and their advice fall in deaf ears, they retreat, leaving the field free to wicked spirits.[14]

Experience proves that, in those who do not profit from the advice they receive from good spirits, spirit communications, after shedding some light on certain subjects for some time, gradually degenerate and fall into error, verbiage or ridicule – an indisputable sign of the absence of good spirits.

---

14 Allan KARDEC, *The Gospel according to Spiritism*, ch. XXIV, nos. 11 and 12.

To obtain the assistance of good spirits, to banish irresponsible and lying spirits, such must be the firm goal and constant effort of all serious mediums; otherwise, mediumship turns into a sterile faculty, which can even become detrimental to those who possess it, should it degenerate into a dangerous obsession.

Mediums that understand their duty, instead of boasting of a faculty which does not belong to themselves, since it can be taken away from them, relate to God all the good things they accomplish. If their communications deserve praise, such mediums are never vain, because they know that the communications are independent of their personal merit, and instead they thank God for allowing good spirits to communicate through them. If they give rise to criticism, they do not take offence, because such messages are not the work of their own soul. Deep inside, they tell themselves that they have not been a good instrument, and that they still do not have all the necessary qualities to oppose the interference of evil spirits; that is why they seek to acquire such qualities, by asking through prayer the strength they may lack.

10. Prayer

Almighty God, allow good spirits to assist me in the communication that I request. Preserve me from the presumption of believing that I am safe from evil spirits; from the pride that could deceive me about the worth of what I am about to obtain; and any feelings contrary to charitable love toward other mediums. If I am misled, inspire someone to warn me, and myself to be humble in accepting their criticism with gratitude, and to take firstly for myself, and not for others, the advice that the good spirits will dictate to me.

If I am tempted to abuse anything, or to take pride in the faculty that you willed to grant me, I beg you, O Lord, to withdraw it from me, rather than allow it to be diverted from its providential purpose, which is the good of each and every one, and my own moral advancement.

2
Prayers for oneself

To Guardian Angels and Protector Spirits

11. Introduction

We all have a good spirit that has been attached to us since our birth and has taken us under its protection. It fulfills with us the mission of a parent toward its child, namely, to lead us to the path of good and progress through life's trials. It is happy when we respond to its solicitude; deeply unhappy when it sees us fall.

Its name is of little relevance to us, for it may have no known name on earth. So we invoke it as our guardian angel, our good guardian spirit. We may even invoke it under the name of any higher-order spirit with which we feel a particular affinity.

Besides our guardian angel, which is always a Higher-order Spirit, we have protector spirits that, regardless of being less elevated, are none the less good and benevolent. They usually are our deceased parents, or friends, or sometimes persons whom we have not known in our current lifetime. They assist us with their advice, and often by intervening in the acts of our life.

Sympathetic spirits[15] are those which attach themselves to humans by a certain similarity of tastes and inclinations; they may be good or bad, according to the nature of inclinations that draw them to us.

Tempting spirits strive to deduce us and divert us from the path of goodness by suggesting bad thoughts. They take advantage of all our weaknesses as open doors that give them access to our souls. There are some that go after us like prey, but *they go away when they realize they are unable to fight against our will.*

God has given us a main higher-order guide in our guardian angel, and secondary guides in our protector and familiar spirits; however, it is a mistake to believe that we necessarily have an evil spirit placed near us to counterbalance the good influences. Evil spirits come voluntarily, according to whether they find fault with us in our weaknesses, or our negligence in following the inspirations of good spirits. It is therefore we ourselves who attract them. As a result, we are never deprived of the assistance of good spirits, and it is up to us to ward off the bad ones. By its imperfections, human beings are always the first cause of the miseries they

---

15 [Trans. note] That is, *affinity spirits*.

endure; and most often they themselves are their own evil spirits.[16]

A prayer to guardian angels and protector spirits should aim at appealing to them to intervene with God, to ask God the strength to resist evil suggestions; and also for assistance in coping with life's necessities.

12. Prayer

Wise and kind spirits, messengers of God, whose mission is to assist humans and to lead them in the right way, support me through my life's trials and tribulations; give me the strength to bear them without grumbling. Turn away from me any evil thoughts, and make it so that I do not grant bad spirits, which would try to induce me to evil, any access to my soul. Enlighten my conscience regarding my faults, and remove from my eyes the veil of pride that could prevent me from seeing them and confessing them to myself.

You especially, ... [insert name], my guardian angel, which especially watches over me; and you all, protector spirits, that seem to have an interest in me, make me worthy of your kindness. You know my needs, let them be satisfied according to the will of God.

---

16 Allan KARDEC, *The Gospel according to Spiritism*, ch. v, no. 4.

13. (ANOTHER prayer)

God, allow the good spirits that surround me to come to my aid when I am in pain, and to support me when I stumble. Enable them, O Lord, to inspire me with faith, hope, and charitable love. May they be for me a support, a hope and a proof of your mercy. Finally, let me find next to them the strength I lack in life's trials and, in order to resist evil suggestions, the faith that saves and the love that comforts.

14. (ANOTHER prayer)

Beloved spirits, my guardian angel, you that God in its infinite mercy allow to watch over human beings, be my protectors in the trials of my earthly life. Give me strength, courage and acceptance. Inspire me with all that is good, keep me from sliding down on the slope of evil. May your sweet influence penetrate my soul; let me feel that a devoted friend is there, near me, sharing in my joys and sorrows.

And you, my good guardian angel, never forsake me, for I need your protection to bear with faith and love the trials that God has willed to send me.

To ward off evil spirits

15. "WOE TO YOU, scribes and Pharisees, hypocrites! For you tithe mint and dill and cumin, and have neglected the weightier matters of the law: justice and mercy and faithfulness. These you ought to have done, without neglecting the others. You blind guides, straining out a gnat and swallowing a camel! Woe to you, scribes and Pharisees, hypocrites! For you clean the outside of the cup and the plate, but inside they are full of greed and self-indulgence. Woe to you, scribes and Pharisees, hypocrites! For you are like whitewashed tombs, which outwardly appear beautiful, but within are full of dead people's bones and all uncleanness. So you also outwardly appear righteous to others, but within you are full of hypocrisy and lawlessness." (Matthew 23:23–27)

16. Introduction

Evil spirits go only where they can satisfy their wickedness. In order to keep them away, it is not enough to ask for them to do, or even to command them: we must take away from ourselves whatever attracts them. Evil spirits sniff the wounds of one's soul, as flies scour the wounds of one's body. Just like you cleanse the body to avoid vermin, cleanse the soul of its impurities to avoid evil spirits. As we live in a world where evil spirits abound, good qualities of the heart do not always protect you from their attempts, but they give you the strength to resist them.

17. Prayer

In the name of Almighty God, let evil spirits depart from me, and let the good ones serve as a bulwark against them!

Evil spirits that inspire human beings with bad thoughts; wicked and lying spirits that deceive them; mocking spirits, that play with human credulity, I reject you with all the strength of my soul and close my ears to your suggestions – yet I call on you the mercy of God.

Good spirits that deign to assist me, give me the strength to resist the influence of evil spirits, and the necessary lights not to be deceived by their trickery. Preserve me from pride and presumption; remove from my heart any traces of jealousy, hatred, malevolence, and all feelings contrary to charitable love, which leave as many doors open to the spirit of evil.

To ask for a fault to be corrected

18. Introduction

Our bad instincts are the result of imperfections of our own spirit, and not of our physical organism, otherwise we would escape all responsibility. Our improvement depends on us: every human being who has the enjoyment of their faculties also have, in all things, the freedom of choosing to do it or not to do it – to do good, a person lacks only the will.[17]

19. Prayer

You have given me, O God, the intelligence necessary to distinguish what is good from what is evil. So as long as I recognize that something is wrong, I am guilty of not trying to resist it.

Preserve me from pride which could prevent me from perceiving my faults, and evil spirits which could incite me to persevere in them.

Among my imperfections, I admit that I am particularly inclined to ... [name of imperfection], and if I do not resist this practice, it is because of the acquired habit of yielding to it.

---

17 Allan Kardec, *The Gospel according to Spiritism*, ch. xv, no. 10; ch. xix, no. 12.

Because you are righteous, you have not created me guilty, but rather with equal abilities to do right or wrong. If I followed the wrong way, it is as a consequence of my own free will. But for the same reason that I have the freedom to do evil, I am also free to do good, therefore I have the right to change course.

My current faults are a remnant of imperfections that I have retained from my previous lives; they are my original sin, so to speak, which I can get rid of by my willpower and with the help of good spirits.

Good spirits that protect me, and especially you my guardian angel, give me the strength to resist evil suggestions, and to emerge victorious from this struggle.

Faults are like barriers that separate us from God; and every fault we overcome is a step forward in getting closer to It.

The Lord, in its infinite mercy, deigned to grant me this current lifetime for my advancement. Good spirits, help me make the most of it, so that it does not end up wasted and lost to me; and that, when it pleases God to withdraw me from it, I am better off than when I entered it.[18]

---

18 *Op. cit.*, ch. v, no. 5; ch. xvii, no. 3.

To ask for strength to resist temptations

20. Introduction

Every evil thought can have two sources: one is our own imperfection coming from our soul, the other, a pernicious influence acting upon it. The latter case is always a sign of weakness which makes us vulnerable to this sort of influence, and consequently of being an imperfect soul, in such a way that the one who succumbs cannot blame the influence of an extraneous spirit, since *that spirit would not have come near that person for evildoing, if it had deemed the latter to be inaccessible to temptation.*

When a bad thought rises in us, we can imagine a malicious spirit soliciting us to evil, and to which we are equally free to yield or resist just as if it were the solicitation of a living person. At the same time, we must seek help from our guardian angel, or from a protector spirit, which, in turn, will fight the bad influence in us, looking forward to *the final decision that we are going to make*. Our hesitation in doing evil is the voice of a good spirit that our conscience is able to hear. We recognize that a thought is bad when it turns away from charitable love, which is the basis of all true morals. When instead it is rooted in pride, vanity or selfishness; when its realization may cause detriment to others; and lastly, when it asks us to do unto others what we would not have them do unto us.[19]

21. Prayer

Almighty God, do not let me give way to the temptation that will make me falter. Benevolent spirits that protect me, turn this evil thought away from me, and give me the strength to resist the suggestions of evil. If I succumb, I will fully deserve to make atonement for my fault in this lifetime and in another one, because I will have acted of my own free will.

---

19 See section no. 15 above and Allan KARDEC, *The Gospel according to Spiritism*, ch. xv, no. 10.

Thanksgiving for having overcome a temptation

22. Introduction

Whoever has resisted a temptation owes it to the assistance of the good spirits whose voices he or she listened to. They must thank God and their guardian angel.

23 Prayer

I thank you, God, for allowing me to emerge victorious from the battle I have just fought against evil; make this victory give me strength to resist new temptations.

And my guardian angel, I thank you for the assistance you gave me. May my acquiescence merit your protection again!

Prayer for asking advice

24. Introduction

When we are undecided about doing or not doing something, first we should ask ourselves the following questions:

1) Can this thing I am hesitant to do be detrimental to someone else?
2) Will it be useful to anyone?
3) Would I be glad if someone did this thing to me?

If the thing concerns only oneself, it is advisable to arrive at a balance between the sum of personal benefits and inconveniences that may arise from it.

If it concerns other people – and if by doing good to one it may harm another – one must also weigh in the sum of good and evil in order to abstain from it or to act.

Finally, even for the best things, we must still carefully consider the opportunity and the incidental circumstances, because a good thing in itself can have bad results in disqualified hands, or if it is not conducted with caution and circumspection. Before undertaking it, it is advisable to check its forces and its means of execution.

In any case, one can always ask the assistance of their Protector Spirits by keeping this wise motto in mind: "When in doubt, abstain." (See no. 38 below.)

25. Prayer

In the name of God Almighty, good Spirits that protect me, inspire me with the best resolution to make in the uncertainty where I am right now. Direct my thoughts toward goodness, and turn away the influence of those who try to mislead me.

In life's tribulations

26. Introduction

We can ask God for earthly favors, and God may grant them to us when they have a useful and serious purpose; but as we judge the utility of things from our point of view – and our view is limited to the current time – we do not always see the bad side of what we want. God, who sees better than us, and wants only our good, may therefore refuse to grant them to us, as a parent deny a child anything that could harm him or her. If what we ask is not granted to us, we must not feel discouraged in any way; on the contrary, we should see the deprivation of what we wish to obtain as a test or an atonement, whose reward will be proportional to the resignation with which we bear it.[20]

27. Prayer

Almighty God, you that see our miseries, deign to listen favorably to the wishes that I am expressing to you at this very moment. If my request is inconsiderate, please forgive me; but if it is deemed reasonable and useful, may the good spirits that execute your will help me fulfill it.

---

20 Allan KARDEC, *The Gospel according to Spiritism*, ch. XXVII, no. 6; II, nos. 5, 6, 7.

Whatever the outcome, my God, may your will be done. If my wishes are not answered, it is because it is in your plans to test me, and I submit without grumbling. Make me not feel discouraged, and that neither my faith nor my resignation be shaken.

... [insert request].

Thanksgiving for a favor obtained

28. Introduction

We should not consider only things of great importance as being worthy of celebration; often apparently trivial events and experiences are the ones that most affect our destiny. Humans easily forget good, preferring to remember grief instead. If, day by day, we recorded the benefits of which we have been the target without even asking for them, we would be constantly taken aback by their great number, which are often erased from our memory by neglect and ingratitude.

Every night, when lifting our souls to God, we must remember within ourselves all the favors It has bestowed upon us during the day, and thank It for them. It is especially at the very moment when we feel the effect of God's goodness and protection that, by a spontaneous impulse, we must show It our gratitude. For that, it suffices to send God a thought acknowledging the benefit received, without having to turn away from one's work or activity.

God's blessings are not only in material things; we must also thank It for the good ideas and felicitous inspirations that are suggested to us. While the proud takes the merit of them, while the unbeliever attributes them to mere chance, those who have faith gives thanks to God and the good spirits. For doing that, long sentences would be useless: "Thank you, Lord, for inspiring me with a good thought" says more than too many words. The spontaneous impulse that makes us refer to God all that happens to us testifies to a habit of being grateful and humble, which wins over the sympathy of good spirits.[21]

29. Prayer

God of infinite goodness, may your name be blessed for the benefits you have bestowed upon me; I would be unworthy if I ascribed them to chance events or to my own merit.

Good spirits, you that have been the executors of God's will, and especially you, my guardian angel,

---

21 Allan KARDEC, *The Gospel according to Spiritism*, ch. XXVII, nos. 7 and 8.

I thank you all. Ward off from me any thoughts of pride, or of using these benefits for any purpose other than doing good.

Thank you especially for ... [insert favor obtained]

Act of submission and resignation

30. Introduction

When something that causes pain or suffering happens to us, once we seek its cause, we often find that it is the result of our own imprudence, our improvidence, or an earlier action – in this case, we should only blame ourselves. If we took no part whatsoever in the cause of a misfortune, then it is either a test for our current life, or an atonement for a past existence. In the latter case, the nature of the atonement can be indicative of the nature of the fault itself, since we are always punished within the scope of our wrongdoing.[22]

In whatever afflicts us, we generally see only the current evil, and not the subsequent favorable outcomes that it may have. Good is often the result

---

22 *Op. cit.*; ch. v, nos. 4, 6 *et seq.*

of a transient malady, since the healing of a patient is often the result of the painful means employed to obtain it. In any case, we must submit to the will of God, bear with courage all tribulations of life, if we want this to be taken into account, so that this saying by Jesus Christ is applied to us: Blessed are those who suffer.[23]

31. Prayer

God you are sovereignly just; all suffering here below must have a cause and a purpose. I accept the affliction I have just experienced as an atonement for my past faults and a test for the future.

Good spirits that protect me, give me the strength to endure without grumbling. Let it be a salutary warning for me; something that will increase my experience. Let it combat my pride, excessive ambition, foolish vanity, and selfishness, thus contributing to my advancement.

32. (ANOTHER prayer)

I feel, O God, a need to pray to you to give me the strength to bear the trials you have willed to send me. Allow the light to be bright enough in my spirit so that I can appreciate the full extent of a love that afflicts me in order to save me. I submit with resignation, O God; but alas! as your created

---

23 *Op. cit.*; ch. v, no. 18.

being I feel so weak that if you do not help me I am afraid of succumbing. Do not forsake me, O Lord, for without you I cannot do anything.

33. (ANOTHER prayer)

I look up to you, Lord, and I feel strengthened. You are my strength, do not forsake me! I am crushed under the weight of my iniquities! Please help me. You know the weakness of the flesh, and you will not look away from me!

I am devoured by a burning thirst; do sprinkle from the spring of living water, and I will be quenched. May my lips only art to sing your praises and not to grumble in the afflictions of my life. I am weak, Lord, but your love will give me strength.

O Lord Eternal! You alone are great, you alone are the aim and objective of my life. Your name be blessed, if you strike me, for you are the master and I am your unfaithful servant; I will bend my head without a murmur, for you alone are great, you alone are the goal.

In face of imminent danger

34. Introduction

The dangers we incur, serve as a warning of our weakness and the fragility of our existence, as reminded by God. The Lord Eternal shows us that our life is in Its hands, and that it hangs by a thread that can be broken when we least expect it. In this respect, there is no privilege for anyone, for both the mighty and the meek are subject to the same alternatives.

If one examines the nature and the consequences of a danger, it will become clear that such consequences, should they materialize, would most often be the correction for a fault committed or a neglected duty.

35. Prayer

Almighty God, and you, my guardian angel, help me! If I must succumb, may the will of God be done. If I am spared, may the rest of my life be used to repair the harm I may have done and to repent of it.

Thanksgiving for having escaped a danger

36. Introduction

By the danger we have endured, God shows us that we may from one moment to the next be called to account for the use we have made of our life. It is thus that God warns us to look within ourselves, and to amend ourselves.

37. Prayer

God, and you, my guardian angel, I thank you for the help you sent me to deliver me from the peril that threatened me. May this danger be a warning to me, and may it enlighten me on the faults that may have attracted to me. I understand, Lord, that my life is in your hands, and that you can take it away when you please. Inspire me, through the good spirits that assist me, with the thought of constructively use the time that still remains for me to spend here below.

My guardian angel, strengthen me in my resolution to right my wrongs and do as much good as I can, so that I may arrive loaded with less imperfections in the spirit world, when it pleases God to call me back there.

When going to sleep

38. Introduction

Sleep is for resting the body, but the spirit does not need to rest. While the senses are numb, the soul emerges partially from matter, and enjoys its spirit faculties. Sleep has been given to humans for restoring organic forces and also for moral forces. While the body recovers the elements it lost through the activities of the day before, the spirit invigorates itself among other spirits – it draws from what it sees, in what it hears, and in the advice given to it. On awakening, these ideas reappear in the guise of intuition. For the spirit, sleep is the temporary return from the exile to its true homeland; like a prisoner momentarily enjoying freedom.

But it just so happens, as with the unscrupulous prisoner, that the spirit does not always take advantage of this moment of freedom for its own advancement. If it harbors bad instincts, instead of seeking the company of good spirits, it seeks the company of its kind, and goes to places where it can give free rein to its inclinations.

May those who have been penetrated by this truth rise their thoughts when they feel it is time to fall asleep. May they call on the advice of good spirits and those departed whose memory is dear to them. May these spirits come to those who are asleep, during the short interval granted to them; and on waking up, such persons will feel heightened strength against evil, and more courage to face adversity.

39. Prayer
My soul will be with other spirits for a moment. Let those that are good come and help me with their advice. My guardian angel, make me wake up and keep a lasting and healthy impression of these encounters.

When sensing that one's life is coming to an end

40. Introduction
Faith in the future and elevation of thought during life, toward future destinies, help the prompt release of the spirit, loosening the bonds that tie it to the fleshly body – and often bodily life is not even yet extinct that the soul, impatient, has already taken off toward the immensity. In individuals who, on the contrary, concentrate all their thoughts in material things, these bonds are more tenacious, *the*

separation is painful and arduous, and the awakening beyond the grave is full of trouble and anxiety.

41. Prayer

❧ God, I believe in you and your infinite goodness; that is why I cannot conceive that you gave humans intelligence to know you and aspiration for the future only to plunge them into nothingness.

I believe that my body is only the perishable envelope of my soul, and that when it ceases to live, I will wake up in the spiritual world.

Almighty God, I feel myself breaking the bonds that unite my soul to my body, and soon I will be held accountable for the use I made of this lifetime that is now ending.

I am going to reap the consequences of both good and evil that I have done; illusions and subterfuges are no longer possible: my whole past will unfold before me, and I will be judged according to my deeds.

I will not take with me any earthly possessions; any honors, riches, satisfactions of vanity and pride. All that belongs to the body at last will remain here below; not a single parcel will follow me, and none of this will be of the slightest help to me in the world of spirits. I will take with me only that which belongs to the soul, in other words, the good and the bad qualities which will be weighed in the scales of rigorous justice. And I will be judged with even more severity if my position on earth gave me more opportunities to do good than I actually have done.[24]

O merciful God, may my repentance reach you! Deign to extend to me your indulgence.

If it pleases you to prolong my existence, let the remaining time be used by me to repair as much as possible any harm I may have done. But if my hour has inexorably struck, I will take with me the comforting thought that I will be allowed to redeem myself by means of new trials, in order to merit one day the happiness of the elect.

And if it is not for me to immediately enjoy this unalloyed bliss which is the sharing only of the just par excellence, I know that hope will not be forbidden to me forever, and that with work I'll get to that goal, sooner or later, depending on my efforts.

I know that good spirits and my guardian angel will be there, near me, to receive me; in just a little time, I will see them as they see me. I know that, if I have enough merit, I will meet again those whom I have loved on earth, while those whom I am leaving behind here will one day rejoin me, so

---

24 Allan Kardec, *The Gospel according to Spiritism*, ch. XVI, nos. 9.

that we are all reunited forever in the afterlife. In the meantime, I will also be able to come to visit them on earth.

I also know that I will meet again those whom I have offended; may they forgive whatever grievances they still have against me: my pride, my hardness of heart, my injustice; and thus not overwhelm me with shame by their presence!

I forgive all those who have done me wrong or have wished evil on me while on earth. I hold no grudge or hatred against them, and pray to God to forgive them.

Lord, give me the strength to leave behind without regrets the coarse joys of this world which are nothing next to the pure joys of the world beyond which I am going to enter. Therein, for the just, there is no more torment, no more suffering, no more miseries – only the culprits suffer, but even they have hope.

Good spirits, and you, my guardian angel, do not let me fail at this supreme moment. Make the divine light shine in my eyes, in order to revive my faith should it swerve from its path.

Note: See below *Prayers for the sick and the obsessed.*

3

Prayers for others

For someone in distress

42. Introduction

If it is in the interest of the distressed that their afflicting trials follow their course, they will not be shortened at our request; but it would be impiety on our part to feel discouraged because our demand was not granted. Besides, should there be no cessation of the trial, there is always hope of obtaining some other consolation, which attenuates the bitterness of one's situation. However, what is truly useful for those who are in pain is courage and resignation, without which what they endure have no profit for them, because they shall be obliged to go through the same trial all over again. It is therefore toward this end that we must above all direct our efforts, either by calling good spirits to our aid, or by raising the morale of the distressed through counseling and encouragement; or finally through material assistance, if at all possible. The prayer, in this case, can also have a direct effect, transmitting a fluidic current toward the person, in order to strengthen his or her morale.[25]

---

[25] Allan KARDEC, *The Gospel according to Spiritism*, ch. v, nos. 5 and 27; ch. xxvii, nos. 6 and 10.

43. Prayer

O God, whose goodness is infinite, deign to soften the bitterness of the current situation of ... [insert name], if that be your will.

Good spirits, in the name of God Almighty, I beg you to assist this person in distress. If, it is in his/her interest, not to be spared this affliction, make it so, O Lord, that they understand its necessity for their own advancement. Give them confidence in God and in the future that will make them less bitter. Give them also strength not to to despair, for that would make them lose the fruit of their labors, and make their future condition even more painful. Take my thoughts to this person, and may it give them courage in their time of need.

Thanksgiving for a benefit granted to others

44. Introduction

Those who are not dominated by selfishness rejoice in the good that comes to their neighbor, even though they had not asked it by prayer.

45. Prayer

God, be blessed for the happiness that has happened to ... [insert name].

Good spirits, let this person see in it an effect of God's goodness. If the good that happens to this person is a test, let this person be inspired with the thought of making good use of it and not to waste it vainly, so that this good does not turn into detriment for the future.

And you, my guardian angel which protects me and wants my happiness, dismiss from my mind any feelings of envy or jealousy.

Prayer for our enemies and those who wish us evil

46. Introduction

Jesus said: *Love even your enemies.* This saying represents the sublime in Christian charity; but by this Jesus does not mean that we must have toward our enemies the sane tenderness we have for our friends. Through those words, he tells us to forgive their trespasses, to forgive the harm they done to us, and to render them good for evil. In addition to the merit which results from this attitude in the eyes of God, this serves to show true superiority in the eyes of our fellow human beings.[26]

47. Prayer

Dear God, I forgive ... [insert name] the harm he/she did to me and the one he/she wanted to do to me, as I want you to forgive me and that they themselves forgive me the wrongs I may have done to them. If you sent it my way as a test, let your will be done.

Turn away from me, O God, the idea of cursing him/her, and any malicious wishes against them. Make me feel no joy at the misfortunes that may come to them, nor any pain for the benefits that may be granted to them, so that I do not defile my soul with thoughts unworthy of a Christian.

May your goodness, Lord, by extending itself upon him/her, lead them back to better feelings about me!

Good spirits, inspire me with forgetfulness of all evil and the memory of good deeds. That neither hatred, nor resentment, nor the desire to render evil for evil, come into my heart, for hatred and vengeance belong only to evil spirits whether incarnate or discarnate! May I, on the contrary, be willing to extend to him/her a fraternal hand, to render

---

26 *Op. cit.*, ch. XII, nos. 3 and 4.

him/her good for evil, and to help him/her if it is in my power!

To prove the sincerity of my words, I wish that an opportunity be given to me of being useful to him/her; but above all, O God, guard me from pride or ostentation, and from overwhelming him/her with humiliating generosity, which would make me lose any merit of my action. Should I act this way I would fully deserve that this admonition of Jesus Christ were applied to me: "They have received their reward."[27]

Thanksgiving for the good granted to our enemies

48. Introduction

To wish no harm to one's enemies is to be only half-hearted as far as charitable love is concerned. True charity means that we wish them well, and that we are happy with whatever good may happen to them.[28]

---

27 *Op. cit.*, ch. XIII, nos. 1 *et seq.*
28 *Op. cit.*, ch. XII, nos. 7 and 8.

49. Prayer

Dear God, in your justice, you thought you ought to rejoice the heart of ... [insert name]. I thank you on his behalf, despite the harm he has done to me or that he has sought to do to me. If he seized the opportunity to humiliate me, I would accept it as a test for my charitable love.

Good spirits that protect me, do not allow me to regret myself for doing this; turn away all envy and jealousy from me. On the contrary, inspire me with lofty generosity. Humiliation is in evil and not in good, and we know that, sooner or later, justice will be done to each according to their works.

For the enemies of Spiritism

50. "BLESSED ARE THOSE who hunger and thirst for righteousness, for they shall be satisfied. Blessed are those who are persecuted for righteousness' sake, for theirs is the kingdom of heaven. Rejoice and be glad, for your reward is great in heaven, for so they persecuted the prophets who were before you." (Matthew 5:6,10–12)

And do not fear those who kill the body but cannot kill the soul. Rather fear him who can destroy both soul and body in hell (Matthew 10:28).

51. Introduction

Of all freedoms, the most inviolable is that of thinking, which also includes freedom of conscience. To curse those who do not think the same as we do is to claim this freedom for oneself and to refuse it to others; it is to violate the first commandment of Jesus: charity and the love of neighbor. To persecute them for their beliefs is to attack the most sacred right of every individual to believe what is right for oneself, and to worship God as one sees fit. To constrain them to external acts similar to ours is to show that we are more interested in form than in content, more in appearances than in conviction. Forced abjuration has never resulted in faith, it can only generate hypocrisy; it is an abuse of material force that does not prove any truth. *Truth is sure of itself: it convinces instead of persecuting, because it does not need to resort to it.*

Spiritism is an opinion, a belief; even if it were a religion, why should one not have the freedom to call oneself a Spiritist like one has of saying that one is Catholic, Jewish or Protestant, a partisan of this or that philosophical doctrine, of this or that economic system? A belief will be either false or true:

if it is false, it will fall of itself, because error can not prevail against truth once light is made in our intellects; if true, no persecution can make it false.

Persecution is the baptism of all new, great and righteous ideas; it grows with the size and importance of the idea. The fury and anger of the enemies of the idea is because of the fear it inspires them. It is for this reason that Christianity was once persecuted and that Spiritism is persecuted today; with the difference, however, that Christianity was persecuted by the Gentiles, whereas Spiritism is persecuted by Christians. True, the time of bloody persecution has passed, but if one no longer kills the body, one still tortures the soul. Spiritists are attacked even in their innermost feelings, in their most cherished affections. Families are divided, mother excites against daughter, wife against husband. Some even attack the body in its material needs by depriving it of its livelihood to cause starvation.[29]

Spiritists, do not be distressed by the blows that come your way, for they prove that you are in the truth, otherwise you would be left alone, and you would not be struck. It is a test for your faith, for it is according to your courage, to your resignation and to your perseverance that God will recognize you

---

29 Allan KARDEC, *The Gospel according to Spiritism*, ch. XXIII, nos. 9 *et seq*.

seeds germinate in this child until the day he/she can rise up toward you by his/her own aspirations.

Deign to answer this humble prayer, dear God, in the name and merit of the one who said: "Let the little children come to me ..., for to such belongs the kingdom of heaven."

For someone who is dying

57. Introduction

Death agony is a prelude to the separation of soul and body. We can say that at that moment a human being has only one foot in this world, while the other is in the world beyond. This transition is sometimes painful for those who are fond of matter and have lived more for the enjoyments of this world than for those of the world beyond; or whose conscience is tormented by regrets and remorse. Conversely, for those whose thoughts have risen to the infinite, and have detached themselves from matter, the bonds are less difficult to break, and the last moments are not at all painful, as the soul holds to the body only by a thread, while in the other condition, as described earlier, it holds to matter deep roots. In all cases, prayer exerts a powerful action over the process of separation. (See below "Prayers for the sick ....")[32]

---

32 A. Kardec, *Heaven and Hell*, part 2, ch. 1, "The passage."

58. Prayer

Almighty and merciful God, here is a soul that leaves its earthly envelope to return to the spirit world, its true homeland. May it return in peace and your mercy be extended toward it.

Good spirits who have accompanied it to earth, do not abandon it at this supreme moment; give it the strength to endure the last suffering it must endure here below for its future advancement. Inspire it to devote the last glimmers of consciousness which remain in it, or which may momentarily return to it, to repentance for its errors.

Direct my thought, so that its action can make the process of separation less painful for this soul; and that, at the moment of leaving earth, it may carry within it the comforts of hope.

among Its faithful servants, of whom he is doing the counting today, so that each one is rewarded with their due share according to their works.

Following the example left by the Early Christians, be proud to carry your cross. Believe in the word of Christ, who said, "Blessed are those who are persecuted for righteousness' sake, for theirs is the kingdom of heaven.... And do not fear those who kill the body but cannot kill the soul." He also said,"Love your enemies, do good to those who hate you,... and pray for those who persecute you." Show that you are his true disciples, and that Spiritism is good, in doing what he says and what he has done himself.

Persecution will only last for a while; wait patiently for the dawn to rise, because the morning star is already on the horizon.[30]

52. Prayer

Lord, you said through the mouth of Jesus, your Messiah: "Blessed are those who are persecuted for righteousness' sake;" forgive your enemies; "Pray for those who persecute you;" and he himself showed us how to do it by praying for his tormentors. Following his example, dear God, we ask your mercy for those who are ignorant of your divine precepts, the only ones that can assure peace in this world

---

30 *Op. cit.*, ch. xxiv, nos. 13 *et seq.*

and in the other. Like Christ, we say to you, "Father, forgive them, for they know not what they do."

Give us the strength to endure with patience and resignation their taunts, insults, calumnies and persecutions, as trials for our faith and humility. Turn us away from any thought of retaliation, because the hour of your justice will sound for all of us, and we await it by submitting to your holy will.

For a newly born child

53. Introduction

Spirits reach perfection only after having undergone the trials of corporeal life. Those who are still wandering wait for God to allow them to return to a bodily existence, which should provide them with a means of advancement, either by atonement of their past faults by means of the vicissitudes to which they are subject, or by fulfilling a mission useful to humanity. Their advancement and future happiness will be commensurate with the way they have spent their lifetime on earth. The task of guiding their first steps, and directing them toward goodness, is entrusted to their parents, who will answer before God for the manner in which they have fulfilled their mandate. It is to facilitate its execution that

God has made parental love and filial love a law of nature; a law which is never violated with impunity.

54. Prayer (to be said by the parents)

Spirit which has incarnated in the body of our child, welcome to our family. Almighty God be praised for sending it too us.

It is a deposit entrusted to us of which we will have to be accountable one day. If it belongs to the new generation of good spirits that must populate the earth, thank you, dear God, for this favor! If it is an imperfect soul, our duty is to help it progress in the way of good through our counsels and good examples. If it falls into evil through our fault, we will answer for it before you for not having fulfilled our mission as this child's parents.

Lord, support us in our task, and give us strength and willpower to fulfill it. If this child turns out to be cause of hardship for us, may your will be done!

Good spirits that came to preside over this child's birth and that must accompany this child during life, please never give up. Ward off from this child any evil spirit that may try to induce evil. Give this child strength to resist such suggestions, and the courage to endure with patience and resignation any trials that may beset this child here on earth.[31]

---

31 *Op. cit.*, ch. XIV, no. 9.

55. (ANOTHER prayer)

Dear God, you have entrusted me with the fate of one of your spirits. Lord, make me worthy of the task imposed upon me; give me your protection; enlighten me, so that I may discern at an early age the tendencies of the child whom I must prepare to enter into your peace.

56. (ANOTHER prayer)

Infinitely kind God, since it has pleased you to allow the spirit of this child to reincarnate so as to undergo earthly tests intended to make it progress, give him/her the light, so that he/she gets to know you, and to love you, and to worship you. By your omnipotence, do let this soul regenerate itself at the source of your divine directives. Under the guidance of his/her guardian angel, may his/her intelligence grow and develop, and make him/her aspire to draw increasingly closer to you. May the science of Spiritism be the bright light that will illuminate this child through life's many pitfalls. Finally, may this child know how to appreciate the full extent of your love which causes us to purify ourselves.

Lord, cast a paternal look on the family to which you have entrusted this soul. May they understand the importance of their mission and make the good

4

Prayers for the departed

For someone who has just passed away

59. Introduction

Prayers for spirits that have just left the earth are not only intended as a a testimony of sympathy, but also have the effect of helping them disengage from the body, thereby shortening the period of disturbance which always follow a separation from the body, and make the awakening on the other side calmer. But here again, as in all other circumstances, its effectiveness depends on the sincerity of one's thought, and not on the abundance of words spoken with more or less pomp and ceremony, in which, by the way, the heart often takes no part.

The prayers that come from the heart resound around the spirit, whose ideas are still confused, like friendly voices that gently awaken one from sleep.[33]

60. Prayer

❧ Almighty God, may your mercy spread over the soul of ... [insert name], whom you have just called to you. May the trials that he/she suffered on earth be taken into account, and our prayers soften and shorten the sorrows he/she can still endure as spirit!

---

33 Allan KARDEC, *The Gospel according to Spiritism*, ch. XXVII, no. 10.

Good spirits that have come to receive this soul, and you especially, its guardian angel, assist it in getting rid of its body's matter. Give it light and self-awareness to draw it from the confusion that usually accompanies the passage from bodily life to spiritual life. Inspire it with repentance for the faults it may have committed, and with a desire to atone for them in order to hasten its advancement toward blessed, eternal life.

[Insert name] ..., you have just entered the world of spirits, and yet you are still here among us; you can see and hear us, for there is nothing between you and us than the perishable body which you have just quitted and which will soon be reduced to dust.

You have left the coarse envelope which is subject to vicissitudes and to death, and now you have retained only your ethereal envelope, which is imperishable and inaccessible to suffering. If you no longer live by the body, you live in a spirit life, which is free from the miseries that afflict humanity.

You no longer wears the veil that deprives us of the splendors of future life. Now, you will be able to contemplate new wonders while we are still plunged into material darkness.

You will roam the spiritual plane and visit worlds freely, while we crawl hard on earth, where we still have to inhabit our material bodies, which are like a heavy burden for us to bear.

Infinity's horizon will unfold before you, and in presence of such magnificence you will understand how vain our earthly desires and worldly ambitions are, and the futile pleasures in which humans delight.

Death is only a material separation of a human from his/her fellow beings for a short while. From this place of exile in which the will of God still holds us, and besides the duties we have to fulfill here below, we will follow you with our thoughts until we are allowed to join you as you have joined those who preceded you.

If we cannot go up to you, you, on the contrary, can come to us. Come therefore amidst those who love you and that you have loved; support them during life's trials; watch over those who are dear to you. Protect them according to your power, and soften their sorrow with the thought that you are happier now, and of the comforting certainty that, one day, you are going to be reunited in a better world.

In the world where you are, all earthly resentments must disappear. May you, for the sake of your future happiness, be henceforth inaccessible to such feelings! Forgive those who may have done wrong to you, as you are forgiven the wrong you may have done to them.

Note: One can add to this prayer, which is generic, some specific words depending on the particular circumstances of family or relationship, and the position of the deceased.

If the deceased is a child, Spiritism teaches us that it is not a recently created spirit, but rather one that had other lives before this and can already be very advanced. If its last lifetime was short, it was only to complete a previous trial, or it was meant to be a test for the parents.[34]

61. (ANOTHER prayer)[35]

Almighty God, may your mercy be extended to our brothers and sisters who have just left earth! Let your light shine in their eyes, take them out of darkness, open their eyes and their ears! May your good spirits surround them and make them hear words of peace and hope!

---

34 *Op. cit.*, ch. v, no. 21.

35 This prayer was dictated to a medium in Bordeaux (France) at the moment the burial convoy of a stranger was passing right in front of the medium's window.

Lord, however unworthy we are, we dare to implore your merciful indulgence on behalf of our brothers and sisters who have just been taken away from this earthly exile. Let their return to the spiritual world be like that of the prodigal son. Forget, dear God, the mistakes they made, and instead remember their good deeds. Your justice is immutable, we know it well, but your love is immense; we beg you to appease your justice with this source of kindness that flows from you.

May light surround you, my brother/sister, who have just left earth! May the good spirits of the Lord come down to you, surround you and help you break free of your earthly chains! May you understand and see the greatness of our master; submit without grumbling to his justice, and never despair of his mercy. Brother! Sister! Let a serious return to your past open the door to the future by making you understand the mistakes you leave behind, and the work you have to do to fix them! May God forgive you, and may his good spirits give you support and encourage you! Your brothers and sisters down here on earth will pray for you and ask you to pray for them.

For those departed who were dear to us

62. Introduction

How awful is the idea of nothingness! Those are to be pitied who think that the voice of a friend who mourns his or her friend is lost in the void and finds no answering echo! They have never known pure and holy affections, those who think that everything dies with the body; that the genius which once enlightened the world with his/her vast intelligence is a play of matter which is extinguished forever, like a breath of air; or that one's dearest living being, such as a father, a mother, or a beloved child is gone forever, leaving behind just a handful of dust that time will scatter irrevocably!

How could a kind-hearted person remain indifferent to this thought? How does the idea of absolute annihilation not freeze such a person with fright and make him/her at least desire that it was not so? If up to this day his/her reason was not capable to remove their doubts, here is Spiritism, which comes to dispel any uncertainty about the future by means of material proofs that it has given of the survival of the soul and the existence of beings from beyond the grave. Everywhere these proofs are welcomed with joy, and confidence is reborn, for humans now know that earthly life is only a short passage that leads to a better life; that their labors here below are not lost to them; and that the most holy affections are not hopelessly broken.[36]

63. Prayer

Dear God, deign to receive favorably the prayer that I address to you for the spirit of ... [insert name]. Give him/her a glimpse of your divine light, and facilitate for his/her soul the way to eternal bliss. Allow good spirits to carry my words and my thoughts to him/her.

And you who were dear to me in this world, hear my voice calling you to offer a new pledge of my affection. God has allowed you to be the first to depart: I cannot complain without being selfish, for it would be regrettable to overwhelm you with the sorrows and sufferings of earthly life. I am therefore resignedly awaiting the moment of our meeting again in the happier world into which you have preceded me.

I know that our separation is only momentary, and that, regardless of how long it may seem to me, its duration fades before the everlasting happiness

---

36 Allan KARDEC, *The Gospel according to Spiritism*, ch. IV, no. 18; V, no. 21.

that God has promised to Its chosen ones. May his kindness preserve me from doing anything that may delay this desired reunion, and so spare me the pain of not finding you again. at the end of my earthly captivity.

How sweet and comforting is the certainty that between us there is only a material veil that prevents me from seeing you! That you can be there, by my side, seeing me and hearing as usual, and even better than before; that you have not forgotten me as I myself have not forgotten you; that our thoughts never cease to blend; and that yours follows mine, always sustaining me.

May the peace of the Lord be with you.

For distressed souls requesting prayers for themselves

64. Introduction

To understand the relief that prayer can provide to suffering spirits, it is necessary to refer to the way it performs, as explained elsewhere.[37] Those who are penetrated by this truth pray fervently, because they are absolutely sure that their prayers are not in vain.

---

37 *Op. cit.*, ch. XXVII, no. 9, 18 *et seq.*

65. Prayer

🕯 *Merciful and forgiving God, may your kindness spread over all the spirits that recommend themselves to our prayers, and especially over the soul of ... [insert name].*

Good spirits, whose goodness is your only occupation, intercede with me for the relief of these souls. Make a ray of hope shine in their eyes, and let divine light illuminate them so that they can detect the imperfections which have kept them away from the abode of the blessed. Open their hearts to repentance and the desire to purge themselves, thus hastening their advancement. Make them understand that by their efforts they can shorten the time of their trials.

May God, in Its kindness, give them the strength to persevere in their good resolutions!

May these benevolent words soften their troubles by showing them that there are beings on earth who sympathize with them and wish them happiness.

66. (ANOTHER prayer)

🕯 *We pray you, O Lord, to extend to all those who suffer, whether on the spiritual plane as wandering spirits or among us as incarnate souls, the graces of your love and your mercy. Have pity on our weaknesses. You made us fallible, but you gave us the strength to resist evil and defeat it. May your mercy be extended to all who have not been able to resist their evil inclinations, and are still dragged on a bad path. May your good spirits surround them; let your light shine before their eyes, and that, attracted by its life-giving warmth, they come humbled, repentant, and submissive, falling prostrate at your feet.*

We also pray to you, merciful God, for those brothers and sisters who did not have the strength to bear their earthly trials. You give us a burden to carry, Lord, and we must not lay it down at your feet. However, our weakness is great, and we sometimes lack courage along the way. Have pity on those indolent servants who abandoned work before time; may your justice save them and allow your good spirits to bring them relief, comfort, and hope in the future. The prospect of forgiveness strengthens one's soul. Reveal it, Lord, to those guilty despairing spirits, and they, supported by this hope, will draw strength from the very enormity of their faults and sufferings, in order to redeem their past and prepare themselves to conquer the future.

For a deceased enemy

67. Introduction

Charity towards our enemies must follow them beyond the grave. We must think that the harm they have done to us has been a test for us that may have been useful for our advancement, if we were able to benefit from it. Such a test may even have been more profitable to us than any purely material afflictions, for having enable us to add charitable love and forgetfulness of offenses to courage and resignation.[38]

68. Prayer

Lord, it has pleased you to call before me the soul of ... [insert name] back to the spiritual world. I forgive him/her the harm he/she has done to me, and their bad intentions toward me. May he/she regret it now that he/she is no longer plagued by the illusions of this world.

May your mercy, dear God, spread over him/her, and remove from me any thought of rejoicing at his/her death. If I have done wrong to him/her, forgive me, just as I forgive the wrong this enemy of mine has done to me.

---

38 *Op. cit.*, ch. X, no. 6; XVII, NOS. 5 AND 6.

For a criminal

69. Introduction

If the effectiveness of prayers was proportional to their length, the longest should be reserved for the most culpable individuals, since they need it more than those who have lived saintly. To refuse to pray for criminals shows a lack of charitable love and a gross disregard of God's mercy. To think prayers are useless in this case, because someone has committed such or such a fault, is to prejudge the justice of the Most High.[39]

70. Prayer

O Lord, merciful God, do not repel this criminal who has just left earth. Human justice may have struck him/her, but this does not free him/her from your justice, if their heart has not been touched by remorse.

Raise the blindfold that hides the severity of their crimes. May his/her repentance find grace in your presence, and alleviate the sufferings of his/her soul! May our prayers and the intercession of good spirits also bring him/her hope and comfort; and inspire him/her with the desire of atoning for his/her bad deeds in a new lifetime. Also give him/

---

39 *Op. cit.*, ch. XI, no. 14.

her the strength not to succumb to new struggles he/she will have to face!

Lord, have mercy on him/her!

For someone who has committed suicide

71. Introduction

No human being ever has the right to dispose of his or her own life, for only God has the right to pull one out of earthly captivity when It deems appropriate. However, divine justice can soften its severity regarding its circumstances, although it reserves all its severity for those who have tried to escape the trials of life. A suicide is like the prisoner who escapes from his prison before the expiration of his sentence, and who, when captured again, is held more severely. This is what happens to a suicide, who thinks to have escaped current miseries, only to be immersed in greater misfortunes.[40]

72. Prayer

Dear God, we know the fate reserved for those who violate your laws by deliberately abridging their days; but we also know that your mercy has no

---

40 *Op. cit.*, ch. v, nos. 14 *et seq.*

bounds. Deign to extend it to the soul of ... [insert name]. May our prayers and your compassion soften the bitterness of the sufferings his/her soul now endures for not having had the courage to wait the end of his/her life's trials!

Good spirits, whose mission is to assist the unfortunate, take this soul under your protection. Inspire it with regret for its faults, and may your assistance give it strength to endure with more resignation the new trials that it will have to undergo in order to atone for them. Remove from this soul all evil spirits which could again drag it to evil and prolong its sufferings by making it lose the fruit of its labor in future trials.

As for you, whose misfortune is the subject of our prayers, may our compassion soften your bitterness and bring forth in you hope for a better future! This future is in your hands; entrust yourself to the kindness of God, which takes to its bosom all who have repented, remaining closed only to those whose hearts have hardened.

For repentant spirits

73. Introduction

It would be unfair to place in the same category of evil spirits, those suffering and repentant spirits which ask for prayers. They may have been bad in the past but have since changed their ways, and now admit their faults and sincerely regret them. They are only unhappy; some have even begun to experience some relative happiness.

74. Prayer

Merciful God, which accepts the sincere repentance of any incarnate or discarnate sinner, here is a spirit that had delighted in evil, but which has now acknowledged its wrongs and entered the right path. Deign, dear God, to receive this soul as a prodigal son worthy of forgiveness.

Good spirits whose voice it has misunderstood, it will listen to you henceforth. Allow it to have a glimpse of the happiness enjoyed by the elect of the Lord, so that it perseveres in the desire to purify itself in order to attain it. Support it in its good resolutions, and give it strength to resist its bad instincts.

Spirit of ... [insert name], we congratulate you on your change of mind, and we thank the good spirits that helped you!

If you formerly delighted in doing evil, it is because you did not understand how sweet the enjoyment of doing good is. You also felt too low to hope that you could attain it. But from the moment you set foot on the right path, a new light has been made for you; you have begun to taste an unknown happiness; and hope has entered your heart. It is because God always listens to the prayer of a repentant sinner; God rejects none of those who come to It. To recover God's favor completely, apply yourself from now on, not only to do no harm any more, but to do good, and especially to repair the evil that you have done. Then you will have satisfied the justice of God; every good action will erase one of your past mistakes.

The first step is done; now, the further you go, the more gratifying and easier the path will seem. Persevere then, and one day you will have the glory of be counted among the good and the blessed spirits.

For hardened spirits

75. Introduction

Evil spirits are those not yet touched by repentance; which are fond of evil, and conceive of no regrets; which are insensitive to reproaches, reject prayer, and often blaspheme the name of God. It is these hardened souls that, after death, take revenge on humans for the sufferings they endure, and pursue with their hatred those they hated during their lifetimes, either through obsession or some fatal influence.[41]

Among evil spirits, there are two quite distinct categories: those which are frankly bad and those which are hypocrites. The former are infinitely easier to bring back to good than the latter; this category is most often composed of often brute and coarse natures, as we see among incarnate humans, which do evil more by instinct than by calculation, and do not feign or pretend to be better than they are. In them there is a latent potential which must be awaken, which is almost always attained with perseverance, firmness, and benevolence, through counseling, reasoning, and prayer. In mediumship, the difficulty they have in writing the name of God is the sign of an instinctive fear, of an inner voice of conscience which tells them that they are unworthy of it. Those which come to Spiritist seances are on the threshold of conversion, and we can all hope for such spirits: it suffices to find the vulnerable point of their heart.

Hypocritical spirits are almost always very clever, but they have no sensitive fiber in their heart;

---

41 *Op. cit.*, ch. X, no. 6; XII, nos. 5 and 6.

nothing touches them. They simulate all good feelings to gain trust, and are happy when they find dupes who can accept them as holy spirits, and whom they can control as they please. The name of God, far from inspiring the slightest fear, serves them as a mask to cover their turpitude. In the invisible world, as in the visible one, hypocrites are the most dangerous beings, because they act in the shadows without raising any suspicion. They have only the appearances of faith without any sincerity.

76. Prayer

Lord, deign to cast a glance of goodness upon the imperfect Spirits that are still in the darkness of ignorance and do not know you, especially that of ... [insert name].

Good spirits, help us make it understand that by inducing humans to do evil; by obsessing and tormenting them; it prolongs its own sorrows. Make the example of the happiness you enjoy an encouragement to it.

Spirit, which still delights in practicing evil, you have just heard the prayer that we said for you. It should prove to you that we wish to do you good, even if you do wrong.

You are unhappy, for it is impossible to be happy by doing evil; then why then stay in pain when it depends on you to leave it? Observe the good spirits around you, see how happy they are, and whether it would not be more pleasant for you to enjoy the same happiness.

You will claim that it is impossible for you to do that; but nothing is impossible to those who will, for God has given you, as to all his created beings, the freedom to choose between good and evil, that is to say, between happiness and misfortune. Therefore no one is doomed to do evil. If you have the will to do it, you certainly have the one to do good and be happy.

Turn your gaze to God. Just for one moment, lift up to It in thought, and a ray of divine light will come to enlighten you. Say with us these simple words: Dear God, I repent, forgive me. Try repentance and do good instead of doing evil, and you will see that Its mercy will spread over you, and that an unknown well-being will replace the anxieties you now endure.

Once you have taken one step in the right direction, the rest of the way will seem easy. You will then understand how much time you have wasted for your happiness through your faults; but a radiant and hopeful future will unfold before you and make you forget your miserable past full of trouble and moral torture that would be hell for you if it were to last forever. One day will come that these tortures will be such that you will be willing to stop them at any cost; yet the longer you wait, the harder it will become.

Do not think that you will always remain in the state you are in. No, that would be impossible; you have two perspectives before you: either you suffer much more than you do now, or be happy like the good spirits around you. The first alternative is inevitable if you persist in your stubbornness; a simple effort of willpower on your part will be enough to get you out of the bad place where you are. Hurry up, for every day of delay is a day lost for your happiness.

Good spirits, let these words find their way into this backward spirit, so that they may help it come closer to God. We pray in the name of Jesus Christ, who had such great power over evil spirits.

5
For the sick and the obsessed

Prayers for the sick

77. Introduction

Illnesses are part of earthly life's trials and vicissitudes. They are inherent in the relative crudeness of our material nature and the inferiority of the world we inhabit. Passions and excesses of all kinds sow unhealthy things in our body, often hereditary. In more advanced worlds, whether physically or morally, the human organism, in more depurated and less material state, is not subject to these infirmities, and the body is not undermined by the ravages of passions.[42] We must resign ourselves to the consequences of the environment where our inferiority has placed us, until we have deserved to move to a better one. In the meantime, this should not prevent us from doing whatever we can to improve our current condition; but if, despite all our efforts, we cannot succeed, Spiritism teaches us to bear with resignation our temporary evils.

If God had not intended that corporeal sufferings were dissipated or in some cases softened, It would not have put curative means at our disposal. God's

---

42 Allan Kardec, *The Gospel according to Spiritism*, ch. III, no. 9.

thoughtful solicitude in this respect, in line with our instinct of self-preservation, indicates that it is our duty to seek and apply such means.

In addition to conventional medication elaborated by orthodox medicine, magnetism (mesmerism) made us aware of the power of fluidic action. Then Spiritism came and revealed another force in *healing mediumship* and the influence of prayer. (See *Final remarks* at the end of this book)

78. Prayer (for a SICK PERSON)

Lord, you are all righteousness; therefore I must have deserved the illness that you willed to send me, because you never strike without a cause. I rely on your infinite mercy for my healing; please restore my health, and may your holy name be blessed. But if, on the contrary, I must still suffer, let your name be blessed in the same way; I submit without grumbling to your divine decrees, for all that you do can have no other purpose than the good of all created beings.

Dear God, let this sickness be for me a salutary warning, and make me look inward. I accept it as some atonement for the past, and as a test for my faith and submission to your holy will.

(See prayer no. 40 above)

79. Prayer (for a SICK PERSON)

Dear Good, your designs are inscrutable, and your wisdom you have willed to strike --- [insert name] with illness. Cast, I implore you, a compassionate gaze at this person's sufferings, and deign to put an end to them.

Good spirits, ministers of the Almighty, endorse, I pray you, my desire to relieve this person. Direct my thoughts so that they may pour a salutary balm over his/her body and bring comfort to his/her soul.

Inspire him/her with patience and submission to God's will; give him/her strength to bear his/her pains with Christian resignation, so that he/she may not lose the fruit of this trial.

(See prayer no. 57 above)

80. Prayer (for a HEALING MEDIUM)

Dear God, if you deign to use me as unworthy as I am, I might cure this suffering, if that is your will, for I have faith in you. But without you I am powerless to do anything. Allow good spirits to suffuse me with their salutary fluid, so that I may transmit it to this patient; and rid my mind of any thought of pride and selfishness which could alter its purity.

Prayers for the obsessed

81. Introduction

Obsession is a persistent action exerted upon someone by an evil spirit. It presents itself in very different ways, from a mere moral influence without perceptible external signs, to a complete disturbance of one's body and mental faculties. It obliterates all mediumistic faculties; in writing mediumship (psychography), it is detected by the obstinacy of a single spirit to manifest itself to the exclusion of all others.

Evil spirits are found swarming around the earth, because of the moral inferiority of its inhabitants. Their evil action is one of the scourges to which humankind is exposed here below. Obsession, just like illnesses, and all life's tribulations, should therefore be considered as a trial or an atonement, and be accepted as such.

Just as illnesses are the result of physical imperfections which make the body accessible to pernicious external influences, an obsession is always the result of some moral blemish which opens rifts for an evil spirit. A physical cause must be countered by a physical force, whereas a moral cause can only be countered by a moral force. To avoid diseases, the body should be strengthened; to prevent obsessions one must strengthen the soul. Hence the obsessed should always work for his/her own improvement, which is usually enough to get rid of the obsessor without any extraneous help. Such help becomes necessary when an obsession degenerates into subjugation and possession, because then the patient will probably have lost all his/her willpower and free will.

The motive behind an obsession is almost always vengeance exerted by a spirit, which most often originated in a relationship that the obsessed had with the obsessor in a previous existence.[43]

In cases of serious obsession, the obsessed is like enveloped and impregnated with a pernicious fluid that neutralizes the action of beneficial fluids by repelling them. It is this fluid that one must get rid of; but a bad fluid cannot be pushed away by another bad fluid. By an action identical to that of a healing medium in case of a disease, it is necessary to expel the bad fluid by means of a better fluid which produces something similar to the effect of a reagent. This action is mechanical, but this is not enough: it is necessary above all to act upon the intelligent being, the spirit to which one must have the right

---

43 *Op. cit.*, ch. x, no. 6; xii, nos. 5 and 6.

to speak with authority – and such an authority is given only to those who are morally superior. The greater the superiority, the higher the authority.'

But there is still more to be done. To secure deliverance, the evil spirit must be led to renounce its evil designs, and imbued with repentance and a desire to do good, by means of deftly directed instructions, in particular evocations made for the purpose of the spirit's moral education. Thus one can finally have the double satisfaction of delivering an incarnate from an obsession and converting an imperfect Spirit.

This task is made easier when the obsessed, understanding his/her situation, adds his/her own willpower and prayers to the proceedings. That is not so when the latter, fooled by the deceiving Spirit, deludes himself/herself as to the supposed qualities of the one which dominates him/her, and delights in the error in which the spirit plunges him/her. Far from cooperating, such individuals reject all assistance. This happens in the so-called cases of fascination, which are always infinitely more rebellious than the most violent cases of subjugation.[44]

---

44 Allan KARDEC, *The Mediums' Book*, ch. XXIII.

In all cases of obsession, prayer is the most powerful aid against an obsessor.

82. Prayer (for THE OBSESSED)

Dear God, allow good spirits to deliver me from the evil spirit which has become attached to me. If it is a vengeance that it is exerting for wrongs that I have committed against it in the past, then you have allowed this to happen as a correction, and I am suffering the consequences of my own faults. May my repentance deserve your forgiveness and my deliverance! But whatever this spirit's motive, I call your mercy on it; deign to facilitate the path of progress that will deter it from the thought of doing evil. May I, for my part, bring it to better feelings by rendering it good for evil.

But I also know, dear God, that it is my imperfections that make me accessible to the influences of Imperfect Spirits. Give me light to recognize them. Above all, fight in me the pride that blinds me to the truth about my faults.

How unworthy I feel, to have let a malignant spirit take control of me!

Make this debacle of my vanity, dear God, serve me as a lesson in future. May it strengthen me in the resolution I now take of purifying myself through the practice of good, charitable love and humility, in order to raise a barrier against bad influences from now on.

Lord, give me strength to endure this trial with patience and resignation. I understand that, like all other trials, it will eventually help my advancement if I do not lose the fruit of my sufferings by grumbling, since it gives me an opportunity to show you my submission, and to exercise my charitable love toward an unhappy spiritual sibling, by forgiving it the harm it has done to me.[45]

(See prayers nos. 15 *et seq.*; 46 and 47 above)

83. Prayer (for THE OBSESSED)

Almighty God, deign to give me the power to deliver ... [insert name] from the spirit that is obsessing him/her. If it enters into your plans to put an end to this ordeal, grant me the grace of speaking to this spirit with authority.

Good spirits that support me, and you, this person's guardian angel, lend me your assistance, help me get rid of the impure fluid that is wrapped around him/her.

In the name of Almighty God, I adjure the evil spirit which is tormenting this person to withdraw.

---

45 Allan KARDEC, *The Gospel according to Spiritism*, ch. XII, nos. 5 and 6.-

84. Prayer (for THE OBSESSOR)

🙏 *Infinitely kind God, I implore your mercy for the spirit that is obsessing ... [insert name]. Make it catch a glimpse of the divine light, so that he can see the wrong path he has committed. Good spirits, help me make it understand that it has everything to lose by doing evil, and everything to gain by doing good.*

Spirit that enjoys tormenting ... [insert name], listen to me, as I speak to you in the name of God.

If you wish to reflect on it, you will understand that evil cannot prevail over good, and that there is no way you can be stronger than God and the good spirits.

They could have preserved ... [insert name] from any attack on your part. If they did not do it, it is because he/she had to undergo this trial. But when this trial is over, they will take away all influence you may have on him/her; and them the harm you have done to him/her, instead of injuring this person, will have aided his/her advancement, making him/her feel happier. So your wickedness will have been in vain for you, and will turn against you.

God, which is all-powerful, and Higher-order Spirits are his delegates, which are more powerful than you, will be able to put an end to this obsession when they wish, and your tenacity will be broken by their supreme authority. But by the very fact that God is good, It will still leave you the merit of ceasing this obsessive process of your own will. It is a respite being granted to you; if you fail to avail yourself of this opportunity, you will suffer deplorable consequences. Great punishments and cruel sufferings await you. You will be compelled to implore God's mercy and prayers from your victim, who has already forgiven you and prays for you – which is of great merit before God, and will speed his/her deliverance.

So think while there is still time, for the righteousness of God will come upon you as on all rebellious spirits. Remember that the evil you are doing at this moment will necessarily come to an end, while, if you persist in your hardened conduct, your sufferings will incessantly grow.

When you still lived on earth, would you not deem it foolish to sacrifice a great good for a small, fleeting satisfaction? It is the same now as spirit. What do you gain by doing this? The sad pleasure of tormenting someone, which does not prevent you from being unhappy, whatever you may say, and will make you still more miserable.

Besides, see what you have been missing: look at the good spirits around you, and see whether their fate is not better than yours. The happiness they enjoy will be yours to share when you want it. What does it take for that to happen? To implore God, and do good instead of doing evil. I know you can not transform yourself all of a sudden; but God does not ask the impossible; what It wants is goodwill. So try, and we all will help you. May we soon be able to say for you the prayer for repentant spirits, and you no longer be among evil spirits, until you can counted among the good ones.

(See prayer "For repentant spirits," no. 73 above; and prayer no. 75, "For hardened spirits")

Final remarks

THE CURE FOR SEVERE OBSESSIONS requires a lot of patience, perseverance and dedication. It also asks for tact and skillfulness to direct toward good this kind of spirits which are often very perverse, quite hardened and astute, besides being rebellious to the extreme. In most cases, we must be guided by the circumstances; yet, whatever the character or nature of the spirit, it is a certain fact, that one obtains nothing through constraint or threats. All influence depends solely on one's moral ascendancy. Another fact, equally ascertained by experience as well as by logic, is the *complete ineffectiveness of exorcisms, formulas, sacramental words, amulets, talismans, external practices, or any material signs.*

A long-term obsession can cause pathological disorders, and sometimes requires simultaneous or consecutive treatment, whether through magnetic healing or medical therapy, to restore the person"s physical health. Once the cause has been destroyed, there remain the effects to be extirpated.[46]

---

46 About obsessions, see Allan KARDEC, *The Mediums' Book*, ch. XXIII. See also *La Revue Spirite* [*The Spiritist Review*], February and March, 1864; April, 1865.